STEVIE NICKS

What Made Stevie Nicks, Stevie Nicks?

Gary E. Hodder

Copyright © Gary E. Hodder, 2025

All rights reserved. No part of this publication may be reproduced or transmitted in any form or by any means including photocopying, recording or other electronic or mechanical methods without the prior written permission of the publisher except in the case of brief quotations embodied in critical reviews and certain other non-commercial uses permitted by copyright law

TABLE OF CONTENTS

INTRODUCTION

Chapter 1: Desert Child

Chapter 2: The Gypsy and the Guitar

Chapter 3: Dreams of Silver Springs

Chapter 4: Welcome to the Mac

Chapter 5: Rumours and Realities

Chapter 6: The Witching Hour

Chapter 7: Edge of Seventeen

Chapter 8: Love, Loss, and Leather and Lace

Chapter 9: Dances with Demons

Chapter 10: Enchanted Again

Chapter 11: Sister of the Moon

Chapter 12: What Made Stevie Nicks Stevie Nicks?

Epilogue

INTRODUCTION

To tell the story of Stevie Nicks is to wander through a dream. Not the kind that fades in the morning light, but the kind you carry with you, etched into memory by the sound of a voice, the rustle of chiffon, and lyrics that feel like secrets whispered by the soul.

Stevie Nicks didn't just arrive in rock music. She emerged, like a storm rolling over the desert, like moonlight breaking through clouds, mysterious, magnetic, and utterly unlike anyone before her. She was not merely a singer in Fleetwood Mac. She became its spiritual compass, its enchantress, the woman who sang heartbreak like a hymn and made poetry feel like prophecy.

But what made her who she is? That's the question we ask with both awe and hunger. How did a little girl from Phoenix, Arizona, raised in a family that moved too often to grow roots, become the High Priestess of Rock? How did Stephanie Lynn Nicks become Stevie?

This book is not just a chronology of dates, records, or chart-topping hits. It's an excavation of essence. We will explore the winding path that carved Stevie into the icon she is, her beginnings, her battles, her loves, her losses, and the legacy she never planned, but always carried. Because Stevie Nicks was never just a member of a band. She was a movement wrapped in lace and leather. A survivor cloaked in vulnerability. A poet who danced barefoot on the edge of fame and madness. The first time most of the world heard Stevie Nicks, was through a song called "Rhiannon." The year was 1975. Fleetwood Mac had just released their first album with her and Lindsey Buckingham as new members. The track, just over four minutes long, was unlike anything else on the radio.

Stevie's voice was raw, mysterious, filled with the kind of magic you couldn't fake. People didn't just listen to her, they believed her. The song wasn't just a hit. It was a moment. A myth. A spell. That was always the Stevie Nicks effect. She didn't sing at you; she sang to something inside you. Whether she was wailing in "Gold Dust Woman" or unraveling herself in "Landslide," Stevie's voice became a balm for the broken and a beacon for the dreamers.

Her lyrics were deeply personal yet universal. They spoke of heartache, of resilience, of the delicate dance between darkness and light.

But her appeal wasn't just in what she sang, it was in how she existed. With her shawls, her top hats, and her velvet-wrapped mystique, Stevie built a persona that felt ancient and modern at once. She was a woman in full command of her femininity, but never reduced by it.

She was sensual but spiritual, fragile yet fierce. In a world that demanded women pick a box, muse or maker, witch or wife, Stevie Nicks chose none. She became her own category.

To admire Stevie Nicks is to recognize that her beauty is only matched by her bravery.

For all the glitter and gold, her story is one of grit and grief. She survived heartbreak on a global stage, first with Lindsey Buckingham, then with others who became intertwined in her narrative. She battled addiction in the shadows, during years when such admissions were rare and damning. She made decisions women were not supposed to make, walked away from roles she was told to accept, and bore the cost of her choices without apology. She once described herself as someone who was "always surrounded by people, and still felt alone." That paradox, of being idolized but isolated, seen by millions but intimately misunderstood, shaped her songwriting. Her ballads bleed vulnerability, her anthems roar with independence.

Each verse was a message in a bottle from someone both haunted and healing.

Through the decades, Stevie never lost the rawness that made her real. She never polished away the pain, even as the world tried to wrap her in sparkle. Her authenticity became her armor. And for generations of women, especially women who didn't quite fit the mold, she became more than a musician. She became a mirror. A muse. A myth in motion.

Long before it was fashionable to speak of empowerment, Stevie Nicks lived it. Not always cleanly, not without consequence, but with an urgency that demanded attention.

She was a woman writing her own songs, leading her own career, navigating the brutal terrain of male-dominated rock music. She was an artist who refused to be someone else's muse, she was her own. Even as tabloids devoured her love life and critics underestimated her talent, she stood tall on her platforms, unfazed.

She once said, "I never wanted to be a woman in a rock-and-roll band.

I wanted to be a rock-and-roll star." And that's exactly what she became. One of the few women inducted twice into the Rock & Roll Hall of Fame, first with Fleetwood Mac, then as a solo artist. She paved the way for artists like Florence

Welch, Lana Del Rey, Haim, and countless others who cite her as a guiding light.

But even with all the accolades, Stevie has remained… Stevie. Not reinventing herself every few years like other stars, but deepening into herself. She is one of the rare artists who never needed to chase trends because she is a genre all her own. Of course, with great power comes great pain. And in the chapters ahead, we won't shy away from the shadows.

We'll talk about the strained relationships within Fleetwood Mac, the betrayals, the ego clashes, the moments of silence that screamed louder than any lyric. We'll delve into the toll that touring, addiction, and fame took on her body and spirit. We'll examine her complex romantic entanglements, including the marriage she later regretted, and the child she never had.

We'll also explore her spiritual side, her love of mythology, her belief in destiny, and her profound connection to the supernatural. Because Stevie has always walked with one foot in this world and one in another. She sees things others miss. She writes songs that feel like they were delivered through dreams.

Even in her darkest hours, she found ways to transmute pain into poetry. "Gold Dust Woman," for instance, is not just about drugs or heartbreak, it's about survival. "Landslide" isn't just about aging, it's about becoming. Stevie Nicks has made a career out of turning personal truth into collective healing.

What makes someone a legend? Is it the number of records sold? The awards? The outfits? The headlines? Or is it something harder to measure?

Is it the ability to make someone cry with just a line of a song? Is it the way your presence lingers in a room long after you've left it? Is it the way a generation of women picked up tambourines, wrote poems, wore black lace, and felt seen for the first time?

If so, then Stevie Nicks is a legend not because of what she did, but because of what she gave.

She gave us permission to be complex.

To be strong and sensitive, bold and bruised, lonely and loved. She gave us a soundtrack for our lives, and made sure we knew we weren't the only ones navigating landslides.

Stevie Nicks has lived a life of mythic proportions. But myths, by nature, often obscure more than they reveal. They turn people into symbols and flatten their humanity into legend.

This book aims to do the opposite. It seeks to explore the woman behind the myth, the one who wept while writing in her journal, who paced backstage before walking out into a stadium of adoring fans, who lit candles not just for aesthetics but for healing.

We will go back to her roots, trace her rise, examine her scars, and celebrate her survival. We will hear from those who knew her intimately and those who were shaped by her from afar. We will explore her music, her magic, and the mystery that still surrounds her.

Because the question, What made Stevie Nicks Stevie Nicks?, isn't just a riddle about fame. It's a journey into art, into womanhood, into endurance. It's a story about what it means to hold on to your voice when the world tries to drown it out. It's about what happens when you dare to follow the melody inside you, no matter where it leads.

And if there's one thing Stevie has taught us, it's this:

The path to becoming yourself is never straight. It's a landslide, a moonlit road, a long journey through heartbreak and hope. But when you find it, when you really find it, you don't just sing, You soar.

Chapter 1: Desert Child

Long before the spotlight, the stage, or the swirling shawls, there was the desert. And in that sunbaked landscape, where tumbleweeds drifted like silent ghosts and the wind carried stories no one could quite understand, a girl named Stephanie Lynn Nicks first began to dream.

She wasn't born there, not quite. On May 26, 1948, she came into the world in Phoenix, Arizona, under the clear blue sky and the blazing sun. But even that arrival felt more like the beginning of a myth than a moment in time. The desert would mark her, imprint something wild and ancient into her soul, something that would echo in her music and her movement for decades to come.

Her parents, Jess and Barbara Nicks were loving but practical. Jess, a corporate executive, was ambitious and charismatic, a born leader who would climb the ladder of the business world with ease. Barbara, a homemaker, was warm, protective, and gentle, with a dreamy, artistic streak that mirrored something in her daughter. From the beginning, Stevie was different, not strange, not troubled, just... elsewhere. She seemed to float slightly above the ground like her thoughts were always somewhere between this world and another. As a child, she wasn't the loudest or the most rebellious. In fact, she was often quiet, observant, and a deep thinker with a soft heart. But music stirred her like nothing else. Her grandfather, Aaron Nicks, recognized it early. He was a frustrated musician himself and saw in young Stevie a kindred spirit. By the time she was four, he was teaching her to sing old country songs, playing duets with her, and guiding her through melodies with the devotion of a man who knew he was helping something rare take root. He even wanted them to tour together. Jess and Barbara quickly shut that down, protectively, wisely, but the spark had already been lit. Stevie knew then, even in her tiny body, that music could be her world. Not just a hobby or a pastime, but a calling. Something sacred. If there's a single word that defined Stevie's childhood, it might be movement. Because Jess's job required frequent transfers, the Nicks family relocated often, Utah, New Mexico, Los Angeles, El Paso, and eventually the San Francisco Bay Area. Each new city brought new beginnings, new schools, and new faces. It might have broken a different kind of child, made them guarded, resentful, lost. But for Stevie, it created something else: resilience. Adaptability. A deep interior world.

Her notebooks were full of poems and stories, narratives spun from her own feelings of impermanence. With each move, she became more introspective. She learned to rely not on place, but on presence. On herself.

Still, every new town came with its own kind of loneliness. The kind only children understand, the ache of not being known. But it was in these lonely hours that Stevie began to write. Even before she picked up a guitar, she was crafting lyrics, building songs in her mind, writing imaginary love letters to futures that hadn't happened yet. The seeds of her songwriting were being sown in soil that wasn't stable, but it was fertile. There's something deeply poetic about the fact that Stevie's family moved so often. It mirrored her inner life, forever in motion, restless, searching. But if the world outside kept shifting, the one constant was her mother.

Barbara Nicks was a fiercely protective presence in Stevie's life. More than that, she was a quiet feminist, at a time when that word wasn't spoken in suburban households. She told Stevie she could be anything, do anything.

She encouraged her independence, even when it scared her. In many ways, Barbara was the first person to give Stevie permission to be Stevie.

Their bond would remain close for decades. Even when Stevie was topping charts and selling out arenas, she called her mother constantly, sometimes daily.

Barbara was her anchor, her sounding board, the one person who saw the little girl even when the world saw a rock star.

And Barbara didn't want her daughter to be famous. Not because she didn't believe in her, but because she understood the price. She once told Stevie, "You'd better be sure. Because once you go, you don't come back the same." She was right. But there was no stopping what had already begun. By the time Stevie entered high school, she was already forming an identity that would later bloom into her signature style. She wore flowing clothes, wrote poetry, and remained slightly aloof, interested in art, in the story, in the soul. She wasn't a cheerleader. She wasn't the girl who tried to fit in. She was something else entirely.

And yet, despite her otherworldly persona, Stevie wasn't isolated. She had friends. She had crushes. She had a heartbreak. She experienced the full spectrum of teenage emotion, but with a depth that set her apart.

She felt things were hard. And she turned those feelings into words, into fragments of songs, into emotional truths that would later become anthems. She also discovered something else, performance. Music became more than just something she loved. It became a portal. In her teenage band, The Changing Times, she got her first taste of performing in front of an audience. Her voice was still unpolished, but there was something electric in her presence. A pull. People leaned in when she sang.

That magic, the kind you can't teach or explain, was already there.

A Fateful Encounter

And then came Lindsey.

They met in high school. He was a quiet, brooding musician. She was a poetic dreamer. At a party, he played "California Dreamin'," and she harmonized with him instinctively. Something clicked. Something fateful.

It would be years before they became a duo, but that moment planted a seed. Their creative chemistry, raw, volatile, and transcendent, would go on to change their lives and the landscape of music forever.

But for now, Stevie was still just a teenager. Still writing in journals. Still gazing out windows, wondering where life might lead. She didn't know yet that she would become the voice of heartbreak for millions. She didn't know she would one day write songs that people would play at weddings, funerals, and breakups for generations. She didn't know she would survive addiction, fame, loss, and reinvention.

She just knew she had something. A flicker. A fire.

And it began in the desert.

The Making of a Myth

Looking back, it's tempting to find foreshadowing in every detail of Stevie's childhood. The dry wind whispered through El Paso. The sound of her grandfather's guitar. The constant uprooting made her seek solace in the written word.

But her story isn't a straight line. It's a spiral. A dance. A slow-burning evolution of self.

Even now, Stevie often refers to herself as a storyteller first and a singer second. And that makes sense, because storytelling was her salvation long before it became her profession. From the moment she began to understand the world around her, she sought to understand her place in it. Not through facts or formulas, but through feelings. Through metaphors. Through songs.

That's what makes Stevie Nicks so special, not just her voice, not just her lyrics, but her lens. She sees the world in symbols. She finds the divine in the details. And it all began, as many stories do, with a girl who didn't quite fit in, scribbling secrets into spiral notebooks, dreaming of a life big enough to hold all her longing. She was a desert child, yes. But even then, the winds of fate were beginning to swirl.

Chapter 2: The Gypsy and the Guitar

There are turning points in every life, moments that don't feel monumental at the time but later reveal themselves as hinges on which everything turns. For Stevie Nicks, one of those turning points was a party, a song, and a stranger with a guitar. Lindsey Buckingham wasn't a friend. He wasn't even an acquaintance. But that night in the late 1960s, when Stevie harmonized with him on "California Dreamin'," something happened that neither of them could forget. Their voices blended like smoke and silk, her earthy, mystical tone weaving effortlessly through his polished, intricate guitar work.

It wasn't love. Not yet. But it was chemistry. Creative, unmistakable, and rare.

That chance encounter would grow into one of the most iconic and complicated musical partnerships in rock history. But in that moment, it was just a spark, quiet, beautiful, and impossible to ignore.

Stevie didn't pursue music full-time right away. Like many young women of her generation, she was caught between two worlds: the one she was told she should live in, and the one she dreamed of. She enrolled at San José State University, majoring in speech communication, thinking she might become an English teacher. It made sense on paper, she loved words, stories, and language. But it didn't satisfy the restlessness inside her.

Meanwhile, Lindsey had joined a local psychedelic rock band called Fritz. When their female singer left, he recommended Stevie as her replacement. She joined the group, and just like that, music pulled her back in.

The band played covers and opened for some of the biggest acts of the era, Jefferson Airplane, Janis Joplin, and Jimi Hendrix. Stevie stood on stage night after night, watching legends perform, studying them, absorbing the magic. She wasn't a powerhouse vocalist yet. But she had presence. She moved like a mystic, dressed like a bohemian dream, and carried herself with a confidence that felt older than her years.

The Audience noticed. So did Lindsey.

They were becoming something.

As Fritz began to falter, like so many local bands eventually do, Stevie and Lindsey splintered off and formed a duo: Buckingham Nicks.

They moved to Los Angeles in 1971, driven not by certainty but by faith. They had almost nothing, just a mattress on the floor, barely enough money to eat, and one shot at chasing their dream. They took jobs to stay afloat, Stevie waited tables and cleaned houses, while Lindsey stayed home and worked obsessively on music. She wrote lyrics on napkins, in notebooks, on receipts, anywhere she could find space to spill her thoughts. Her writing was rich with metaphor, emotion, and imagery. It was never just "I'm sad" or "I'm in love." It was: "I've been afraid of changing 'cause I built my life around you." She was a storyteller cloaked in mystery. Their debut album, Buckingham Nicks, was released in 1973. It was raw, earnest, and a beautiful introduction to their sound. Though it wasn't commercially successful at the time, it gave them a glimpse of possibility. More importantly, it solidified their dynamic.

Lindsey was the technical perfectionist, the architect of harmonies and guitar layers. Stevie was the intuitive poet, the heart, the soul, the raw nerve. Together, they balanced each other. But even then, there were signs of friction. Lindsey could be controlling, and obsessive about the details. Stevie could be emotional, ethereal, and stubbornly independent.

Their love was real. Their music was magic. But their storm was already brewing.

Stevie had always described herself as a "gypsy." Not in the literal sense, but in spirit. She was a wanderer, restless, romantic, drawn to change. She moved through the world like a character from one of her own songs, half-rooted, half-flying. She wore flowing shawls and velvet capes, not as a fashion statement, but as a form of armor. Her clothes became part of her myth, something that helped her become the woman the music required.

And in those early years in L.A., the gypsy spirit served her well. Every rejection, every setback, every night spent wondering if it would ever work, she turned it into fuel. Into verse. Into resilience. Stevie wasn't just chasing fame. She was chasing the truth. And she believed, deeply, that her voice, her stories, were meant to be heard.
It was 1974 when destiny finally caught up.
Mick Fleetwood, drummer and co-founder of Fleetwood Mac, was looking for a new guitarist. A mutual friend played him some demos, tracks from Buckingham Nicks, and he was immediately impressed by Lindsey's style.
Mick reached out and offered him the job.
But Lindsey had one condition: Stevie came too.
It wasn't a common request, and it wasn't a given. Fleetwood Mac was already a functioning band with its own identity. Adding a singer with a poetic, witchy aura could have been risky. But

something about Stevie, her voice, her vision, her vulnerability, was impossible to ignore.

The band agreed. And in 1975, Stevie Nicks and Lindsey Buckingham officially joined Fleetwood Mac.

The gypsy and the guitarist had found a new home.

Joining Fleetwood Mac changed everything. But even before the fame, before the platinum records and the chaos that would follow, there was something undeniable about what Stevie and Lindsey brought to the band.

Together, they weren't just good, they were cinematic. Lindsey's guitar work was sharp and expressive, and Stevie's vocals soared with emotion. Her lyrics added new depth to the band's sound, coloring it with moonlight and melancholy.

But beneath the music was a love story in collapse.

Stevie and Lindsey's romantic relationship had begun to fracture. The pressure of struggling financially, of chasing a dream that felt just out of reach, had worn them down. Stevie, always sensitive, always seeking connection, felt increasingly distant from Lindsey. And Lindsey, driven and intense, resented what he saw as her emotional need for space and recognition.

Still, they clung to the music.

It became their common language, even when they couldn't speak to each other.

And that duality, the push and pull, the creation and destruction, would define their legacy.

In these formative years, Stevie was still becoming Stevie Nicks. The voice of heartbreak. The priestess of vulnerability. The woman who could channel myth, pain, and femininity into a three-minute masterpiece.

But even then, she was laying the foundation.

She knew what she wanted. She wasn't a background singer. She wasn't an ornament. She was a force. And she was ready to rise.

She once said:

"Even in my lowest moments, I always believed in myself. I always knew I was going to make it. I just didn't know how."

That quiet confidence, that belief in her own voice, is what carried her through those early years. Through the gigs with Fritz, the heartbreak with Lindsey, the rejections, the small apartments, the waitressing shifts, the soul-splitting arguments.

She held her ground. And her guitar.

And she waited for the world to catch up.

Chapter 3: Dreams of Silver Springs

The world knows Rumours as one of the greatest albums in rock history, an unmatched fusion of musical genius, raw emotion, and blistering personal truth. But behind every harmony, every hook, and every haunting lyric, was a band falling apart at the seams. For Stevie Nicks, it was the beginning of both everything she had ever dreamed of and a heartbreak she would never quite outrun.

"Silver Springs" wasn't just a song. It was a diary entry, a closing argument, and a scream into the ether, all wrapped in one. It was a dream deferred, a promise broken, and for Stevie, it became symbolic of what it meant to create something beautiful from pain. This is the chapter where the dream and the dreamer start to drift apart.

By the time Fleetwood Mac entered the studio in 1976 to record Rumours, the band was already in chaos. Christine and John McVie were separating. Mick Fleetwood's marriage was dissolving. And Stevie and Lindsey, well, they were unraveling in the most spectacularly painful way imaginable.

Still living together in the same shared spaces, the former lovers had now become co-workers, collaborators, and ghosts in each other's presence. There was no privacy. No buffer. Just microphones, lyrics, and pain.

But somehow, out of the emotional wreckage, they created art.

Lindsey channeled his feelings into sharp, biting songs like "Go Your Own Way," which burned with resentment and finality. And Stevie? She wrote "Dreams," the band's only No. 1 hit, a moody, floaty track that told her truth with quiet devastation.

But there was another song, one that didn't make the final cut. A song so deeply personal, so searingly vulnerable, that it never quite found its place in the spotlight.

That song was "Silver Springs."

"You Could Be My Silver Springs…"

Stevie wrote it in a flood of emotion, imagining a life that could've been, an alternate reality where love endured and hearts didn't break under the weight of fame and ambition. The song is poetic, yes, but it's also raw. It doesn't hide behind metaphor the way some of her other work does. It's a direct plea to be seen. To be remembered. To say: This was real. You can't erase me.

"Time cast a spell on you, but you won't forget me / I know I could have loved you, but you would not let me."

"Silver Springs" was meant to be her answer to "Go Your Own Way." It was her rebuttal. Her closure. But when it came time to finalize the track list for Rumours, the song was cut.

The official reason? Length. Flow. Practicality.

But Stevie knew the truth: Lindsey didn't want it there. It hit too close. It laid him bare.

She was devastated.

Not just because it was her song, but because it was her truth. And once again, her truth was being shelved.

Though it didn't appear on Rumours, "Silver Springs" refused to fade into obscurity. It hovered over Stevie's career like a phantom limb, absent, yet always present.

She tried to release it on later projects, but the band always blocked it. It was as if the song itself had become dangerous, a reminder of old wounds, unfinished business, and emotions that no amount of success could bury.

For years, Stevie mourned the song.

But in 1997, everything changed.

Fleetwood Mac reunited for The Dance, a live album and performance that brought them all back together, decades later. And this time, "Silver Springs" was finally given its due.

When Stevie took the stage and sang it, she wasn't just performing. She was purging.

She locked eyes with Lindsey during the final crescendo, her voice rising like a wave:

"You'll never get away from the sound of the woman that loves you…"

It was electric. Painful. Beautiful. A moment frozen in time.

And Lindsey, for all his stoicism, looked back at her, and blinked. Because even then, even after all those years, he felt it. The song. The past. The ache.

In that moment, "Silver Springs" became more than a song. It became the moment.

A legacy sealed.

The truth is that Stevie Nicks was always chasing dreams. Dreams of love. Dreams of music. Dreams of being understood. But reality had different ideas.

The cost of her career was steep. She didn't just lose Lindsey. She lost time, space, and sometimes, herself.

There were nights she sat in hotel rooms and cried, not for lack of fame, but for the silence that came after the applause. The voice that said: You're still alone.

She wrote about it constantly.

"Dreams," "Gypsy," "Landslide," and "Has Anyone Ever Written Anything for You", these weren't just songs. They were her reflections, her emotional snapshots, her battle scars. And "Silver Springs" was the wound that never fully closed.

Still, she never gave up the dream.

She kept showing up. Recording. Touring. Pouring her soul into her art.

She knew the world saw her as ethereal and untouchable. But underneath the shawls and platform boots was a woman who wanted one thing more than anything else: to be heard.

"Silver Springs" eventually became a fan favorite. Its story, its absence from Rumours and its resurrection on The Dance, only deepened its mystique. And in many ways, it became symbolic of Stevie herself: the woman who refused to be silenced, even when others tried to rewrite her story.

She once said that losing the song was like losing a child.

And you believe her.

Because when Stevie sings, she's not just performing. She's remembering. She's time traveling. She's taking you with her into a dream that almost came true, but didn't.

And that's the thing about dreams. Some shimmer like gold. Others haunt like ghosts.

But they all make you who you are.

Chapter 4: Welcome to the Mac

Stevie Nicks had stepped into a world of rock legends. She was no longer just a dreamer in a rented room with a guitar, she was a part of something much bigger. Fleetwood Mac wasn't just a band; it was a living, breathing entity, a force forged in the fires of ambition, creativity, and, at times, chaos. And when Stevie walked into that storm in 1975, she had no idea just how much the world was about to change.

The Fleetwood Mac story had already begun long before Stevie and Lindsey Buckingham entered the picture. Founded in 1967 by Mick Fleetwood and John McVie, the band had undergone multiple lineup changes and sound evolutions, from blues rock to the more polished, soft rock that would define their later success. But in 1975, with the addition of Stevie and Lindsey, the band would experience a metamorphosis, one that would catapult them into superstardom. When Mick Fleetwood first reached out to Lindsey Buckingham to join Fleetwood Mac, he was drawn to his innovative guitar work. What Mick didn't expect was that Lindsey would come as a package deal with Stevie. But Lindsey, always protective of his musical partner, made it clear: if he was in, Stevie was in too. Mick, with his characteristic openness to experimentation, agreed. In fact, Fleetwood Mac's leader had little hesitation about the decision, already sensing that Stevie and Lindsey's distinct sound could transform the band. From the moment Stevie Nicks entered Fleetwood Mac, it was clear that something extraordinary was brewing. While Lindsey brought technical brilliance and precision to the group, Stevie offered something less tangible but equally essential: an ethereal presence, a voice laced with vulnerability, and a magnetic charisma. She didn't just sing, she became the emotional epicenter of the band, wrapping listeners in a musical aura that felt both timeless and otherworldly. But it wasn't just the music that was changing. With the arrival of Stevie and Lindsey, Fleetwood Mac's dynamic shifted in ways that would be felt both creatively and personally for years to come. The band's self-titled album, Fleetwood Mac (1975), marked the first time the new lineup was fully realized in the studio. This was the beginning of a new era, not just for the band, but for the music world at large. The album was a critical success, but it didn't yet carry the weight of the monster hit they were about to create. It was only a glimpse of the magic the band could make together.

The sound was lighter, more accessible, more polished. But it was Stevie's voice and lyrics that immediately set them apart. She was no longer just a mystical figure strumming her guitar in a studio apartment. She was now a professional, her artistry honed in the fires of a decades-old band with a complex history.

The release of "Rhiannon," Stevie's breakout single on the album, further solidified her place within Fleetwood Mac. Written in the backseat of a car while traveling through the Bay Area, "Rhiannon" was born out of Stevie's fascination with Welsh mythology and the woman she envisioned as an ethereal, free spirit. The song itself captured the essence of Stevie's soul, her longing, her mystery, and her raw emotional power. The success of "Rhiannon" on the radio marked the moment when Stevie Nicks became more than just an addition to the band. She was its heart, its voice, its spellcaster. The world would never look at her, or Fleetwood Mac, the same way again. But while Fleetwood Mac (1975) marked the beginning of Stevie's rise, it also introduced the first real taste of the complex relationships within the band. The emotional chemistry between Stevie and Lindsey was undeniable, but it was also fraught with tension. Their on-again, off-again romance had been pushed to the forefront, and as Fleetwood Mac began its rise to fame, their personal issues began to spill into the music. It wasn't just a collaboration, it was a battlefield of creativity, love, and resentment.

Stevie's bond with the rest of the band was equally complicated. Mick Fleetwood, the ever-spirited and often erratic drummer, immediately took to her, finding a kindred spirit in her mystical personality. But John and Christine McVie, the band's rock-solid rhythm section, had their own challenges to face, Christine was working through her own relationship breakdown with John while trying to navigate the pressures of being in a high-profile band. As the band moved through the chaotic whirlwind of touring, recording, and living on the road, Stevie found herself at the center of this storm, no longer just a muse or a poet, but a woman caught between love, heartbreak, and the demands of fame.

But one thing became increasingly clear: Stevie Nicks wasn't just in Fleetwood Mac. She was now a force in Fleetwood Mac. By 1976, as the band began recording what would become Rumours, the world would see just how much Stevie had transformed. The album was a perfect storm of creativity, pain, and collaboration. The tensions that had begun to bubble under the surface in the previous year came to a head, and the band channeled that emotional chaos into their music. Stevie's lyrics were laced with her own heartbreak, but they were also laced with a deep understanding of the human experience. The songs on Rumours tapped into a universal feeling of longing and loss. She was a storyteller, weaving emotion into melody, and through songs like "Dreams," "Gold Dust Woman," and "Rhiannon," she became one of the defining voices of the 1970s. But while Rumours cemented Fleetwood Mac's place in rock history, it also proved to be an emotionally tumultuous time for Stevie. As she sang about love lost, heartbreak, and the struggles of maintaining a relationship amidst the pressures of fame, she wasn't just writing music, she was writing her own personal catharsis. And, in doing so, she created some of the most enduring songs of her career. The paradox of Stevie Nicks's role in

Fleetwood Mac was that she wasn't just a star, she was part of a collective. As much as she was Stevie Nicks, the iconic rock figure, she was also part of the fabric of Fleetwood Mac. Each band member brought something unique, and it was in their collective magic that the band thrived.

Stevie was more than a backing vocalist, more than a mystical force on stage. She was the alchemist who turned pain into art, the artist who spoke to the depths of longing and loss, the woman whose voice could shatter hearts and make them whole again. The band's mix of turmoil, chemistry, and creative genius gave birth to songs that defined an era and transcended genres. It's in this era of Fleetwood Mac's history that Stevie began to truly become the Stevie Nicks we know today, the confident, magnetic figure wrapped in flowing shawls, who had the courage to bare her soul to millions. The woman who would go on to build a legacy that was defined not just by the records she sold but by the emotions she evoked and the lives she touched. Stevie Nicks had found her place in the world, and it was on the stage of Fleetwood Mac.

Chapter 5: Rumours and Realities

In 1977, Fleetwood Mac was on the precipice of something monumental. The band's self-titled album had already solidified their place in rock history, and the follow-up, Rumours, was expected to take them even higher. No one, least of all the band themselves, could have anticipated just how powerful and defining Rumours would become. For Stevie Nicks, it was a period of unthinkable highs and devastating lows. The album was as much about personal revelation as it was about musical brilliance, and it became a mirror to the fractured relationships that were unraveling within the band.

But Rumours was more than just an album, it was a cultural phenomenon. It was a masterclass in songwriting, capturing the deep emotional currents that were swirling beneath the surface of the band's personal lives. It became an anthem for anyone who had ever experienced heartache, longing, and the bittersweet complexities of love. When Fleetwood Mac entered the studio to begin working on Rumours, the band was already a ticking time bomb. The emotional drama that had begun when Stevie and Lindsey Buckingham joined the band in 1975 had only escalated. The two were still deeply in love, but their relationship was on the rocks, torn apart by the pressures of fame, infidelity, and the constant proximity of their personal and professional lives. Meanwhile, Mick Fleetwood's marriage was in disarray, and Christine McVie was going through her own struggles with her now-estranged husband, John McVie. The band's dynamic was one of chaos, passion, resentment, and creative genius all colliding in the most explosive of ways. But within that turmoil came Rumours, an album that was fueled by the very real pain and fractured relationships within the group.

For Stevie, this time in the studio was as much about healing as it was about creation. She poured her heart into her lyrics, writing songs that not only chronicled her own heartbreak but also served as a reflection of the collective turmoil the band was experiencing. Rumors became the soundtrack of her pain, a cathartic release of emotions that were too intense to suppress. It was during the making of Rumours that Stevie Nicks wrote some of her most iconic songs, including "Dreams," "Gold Dust Woman," and "Rhiannon." Each track carried its own weight, telling stories of love lost, betrayal, and personal awakening.

"Dreams" was perhaps the most emblematic of Stevie's emotional journey during this time.

Written after a particularly tense and emotionally charged argument with Lindsey Buckingham, "Dreams" was Stevie's moment of clarity amidst the storm. The song is hauntingly simple yet profound, capturing the resignation and hope that accompanies the end of love. The lyrics, "Thunder only happens when it's raining / Players only love you when they're playing," encapsulated the complexities of their relationship, as well as the overall vibe of Fleetwood Mac during the making of the album.

The song was born out of pain, but it also carried the shimmer of release and reflection. It was Stevie's way of telling the world that she had accepted the inevitable end of a chapter in her life, even if that meant walking away from someone she once thought she couldn't live without.

Then there was "Gold Dust Woman," a track that painted a darker picture of Stevie's inner world.

In a sense, it was the flip side of "Dreams", a song about struggling to find peace amidst the madness, about searching for solace in the midst of self-doubt and emotional destruction.

"Gold Dust Woman" speaks to Stevie's experience with fame, her struggles with substance use, and her battle with loneliness. The lyrics, "Well, I hear you're doing fine / But I hear you're doing fine / But I've got something to say / It's just the things you do that make it feel this way" reveal a sense of disillusionment and isolation.

But while these songs were born from heartbreak, they were also laced with Stevie's strength. She might have been reeling from the breakup with Lindsey, but she wasn't defeated. She was finding her voice, and she was doing so in a way that would resonate with millions of people across the world.

While Rumours soared to commercial heights and cemented Fleetwood Mac's place in music history, the toll it took on the band members, especially Stevie, was immeasurable. Success had come at a steep price.

The band's emotional fallout was only exacerbated by their constant presence in the public eye. The lines between personal and professional life had become increasingly blurred, and the emotional baggage they carried with them began to seep into their performances and interviews. They were no longer just a band; they were a soap opera, with each member of Fleetwood Mac becoming a character in their own personal drama.

For Stevie, this public scrutiny was particularly challenging. As a woman in rock, she was already fighting to carve out her own space in a male-dominated industry. But now, she was being asked to not only be the face of Fleetwood Mac but to also bear the weight of the band's internal battles. She had to reconcile the woman she was becoming with the persona that was thrust upon her.

On stage, Stevie was magnetic. She had become one of the most captivating performers of the era, draped in flowing shawls and boots, commanding attention with every word and every move. Offstage, however, she was struggling. The fame that had once been a dream was now a double-edged sword, leaving her feeling exposed and vulnerable.

The tension between her personal life and the success of Rumours reached a boiling point during the subsequent tour. Stevie and Lindsey's volatile relationship was on full display, awkward silences, emotional outbursts, and passive-aggressive interactions were part of the fabric of their live performances. Yet, despite the personal turbulence, they still managed to create magic on stage, delivering unforgettable renditions of "Go Your Own Way," "Landslide," and, of course, "Dreams."

Despite the behind-the-scenes turmoil, Rumours went on to become one of the best-selling albums of all time. It sold over 40 million copies worldwide and produced some of the most enduring hits in rock history. The band's vulnerability and emotional openness resonated

with listeners, who saw themselves reflected in the heartbreak and longing of the songs.

For Stevie, Rumours represented a turning point. It was the album that solidified her as a force to be reckoned with, not just within Fleetwood Mac, but as a solo artist and a woman in the music industry. The success of Rumours gave her the platform to explore her own voice, both as a member of Fleetwood Mac and as an artist in her own right.

But the reality was that the success of Rumours came at a personal cost. Stevie's relationship with Lindsey, once the cornerstone of her life, was splintering, and the pressures of fame were beginning to take their toll. As she poured her heart into her music, she was also grappling with the realities of her personal life, trying to maintain a sense of self amidst the whirlwind of success.

As Stevie looked out over the sea of adoring fans at Fleetwood Mac's shows, she realized that Rumours had done more than just catapult them into rock history. It had turned her into an icon.

But with that fame came a constant struggle to stay true to herself, to not be consumed by the very thing that had made her a star.

She was no longer just a woman in a band. She was Stevie Nicks, the voice of a generation, the mystical rock star, the woman who had survived heartbreak and turned it into gold. But behind the glittering facade was a woman who was still struggling with the complexities of love, loss, and the demands of fame.

For Stevie, Rumours was more than just an album. It was a reflection of her deepest truths, a snapshot of a time in her life when everything, love, music, and identity, was in flux. The songs that came out of those turbulent years would shape the course of her career and become the soundtrack for generations of listeners who understood the heartbreak she had so masterfully captured.

And though the band's personal dramas would continue to unfold, Rumours was a moment when Fleetwood Mac, and Stevie Nicks, reached the pinnacle of their power.

Chapter 6: The Witching Hour

The world saw Stevie Nicks as a rock star, an ethereal figure draped in flowing shawls, standing in front of a microphone with an almost otherworldly presence. But beneath the glamour and fame lay a woman deeply attuned to the mystical and the spiritual, someone who believed in forces beyond the physical world. The persona of "the witch" was not just an image, it was a reflection of Stevie's very soul, a place where her artistry, intuition, and spirituality converged. In the 1970s and 1980s, as Fleetwood Mac soared to unprecedented heights, Stevie Nicks found herself at the center of a cultural revolution. Her mystical persona, characterized by her flowing garments, dramatic performances, and captivating presence, became a symbol of something deeper, a connection to the unseen, to the magic that could not be explained by conventional means. The "Witching Hour" was not just the time of night when the veil between the worlds was thinnest, but also the metaphorical hour when Stevie Nicks truly came into her own as an artist, a symbol, and a woman. Stevie's relationship with the mystical began long before Fleetwood Mac. Growing up in California, she had always been drawn to the supernatural and the unknown. The family home in the suburbs of Los Angeles was steeped in a sense of spiritual awareness, and Stevie's grandmother, who was a spiritual guide to Stevie, introduced her to the idea of mysticism and the occult at an early age. This early exposure to spiritual practices would later have a profound impact on Stevie's artistry and how she presented herself to the world.

For Stevie, the mystical wasn't something to be feared, it was something to be embraced. She saw herself as a woman not only in tune with the spiritual but one who had the ability to channel these energies into her music. In her world, the lines between the real and the imagined were blurred, and it was this intersection that allowed her to connect with her audience in such a profound way. Her songs, like "Rhiannon" and "Gold Dust Woman," were more than just reflections of her life, they were channels for her spiritual beliefs, her inner world, and the stories of the mystical figures she felt connected to.

The figure of Rhiannon, the Welsh witch and goddess, became one of Stevie's most iconic creations. It was a character that embodied the spirit of independence, mystery, and freedom, qualities Stevie herself embodied and aspired to. "Rhiannon," the song, became not just a hit, but an anthem for the mystical side of Stevie, a persona that the public would come to recognize and adore. And yet, for Stevie, Rhiannon was not just a character, it was a reflection of herself, a spiritual alter ego that allowed her to explore themes of power, loss, and freedom. Through Rhiannon, Stevie could express a part of her soul that was untethered from the constraints of everyday life. Stevie's performances were nothing short of mesmerizing. With her dramatic presence, signature twirls, and flowing black shawls, she became an icon of stagecraft, a woman who seemed to transcend time and space. Her movements were deliberate and hypnotic as if she were casting a spell with every gesture. And perhaps, in some ways, she was. For Stevie, performance was not simply about playing music; it was about creating an experience, one that allowed the audience to connect with her on a deeper, almost mystical level. The "Witching Hour" on stage was a space where Stevie could fully embody the magic that was so intrinsic to her being. When she sang, she wasn't just performing; she was invoking something beyond the music itself. The rituals she performed on stage, her movements, the way she gestured, her posture, were part of a larger spiritual practice that connected her to her fans and to the universe. She understood the power of symbolism, the way certain gestures or moments on stage could create a profound emotional response. In interviews, Stevie often spoke about her connection to the supernatural and how it influenced her music and performances. She believed that her artistry was an extension of her spiritual beliefs, and she saw herself as a channel for these energies. As the "witch," she wasn't simply putting on a costume; she was embodying a persona that allowed her to access parts of her consciousness that would otherwise remain hidden. Her songs were more than lyrics, they were prayers, and invocations to forces beyond this world, and her performances were rituals, crafted to evoke emotions and energies that were timeless. The media, of course, was captivated by Stevie's mystical persona. In a world where women in rock were often reduced to being either muses or temptresses, Stevie Nicks stood out as something entirely different, she was a figure of power, autonomy, and mystique. The press seized upon her witchy image, often emphasizing her connection to the occult and the supernatural. Her outfits, her unique voice, and her persona all seemed to weave together into a compelling narrative that had little to do with the traditional female rock star archetype.

However, this public image was not something Stevie had crafted for effect, it was a reflection of who she was, both as an artist and as a person. The witch persona became part of her mystique, but it also allowed her to confront her own vulnerabilities. The witch was both an embodiment of strength and a symbol of the fragility that lay beneath. She was a woman who was deeply in tune with her emotions, her psyche, and her spiritual self. The witch, in a sense, was her armor, allowing her to navigate the trials and tribulations of fame while still staying true to her creative and spiritual core.

But the witch image was not without its complexities. As the public's fascination with Stevie grew, so too did the pressure on her to maintain the persona. In interviews, she began to address the contradictions inherent in her image. She spoke about how she was often misunderstood, and how the public's perception of her as an ethereal, untouchable figure did not necessarily align with her reality. The truth was that Stevie was both the witch and the woman, she was the person who could conjure magic on stage, but she was also the person who struggled with loneliness, heartache, and the burdens of fame. Behind the scenes, the "Witching Hour" was not always a time of glamour and grace. Stevie was grappling with the pressures of fame, the loss of relationships, and her increasing dependence on drugs and alcohol to cope with the emotional demands of her life. The same magical figure who captivated millions was also wrestling with inner demons, trying to find balance in a world that often felt overwhelming. The witch, in some ways, became a mask that allowed Stevie to protect herself from the harsh realities of life on the road.

Her struggles with addiction during this period were well-documented, but they were also a part of her ongoing battle to maintain a sense of control over her life and her art. Music became a form of therapy for Stevie, an outlet through which she could explore her pain, her grief, and her desire for transformation. The witch, with her mystical powers, became a way for Stevie to reclaim her agency in a world that often seemed to demand too much from her. The witch's role in Stevie's life, then, was both empowering and disempowering. It allowed her to project a sense of strength and mysticism to the world, but it also became a barrier between her true self and the public. The Witching Hour, for Stevie, was both a time of great creativity and intense vulnerability. Today, the image of Stevie Nicks as a witch, as a mystical rock star, is one of the most enduring aspects of her legacy. It is a persona that has become synonymous with her identity as an artist and has shaped her public image for decades. Yet, it is important to remember that Stevie Nicks was never just the "witch", she was, and is, a multifaceted woman with a profound connection to her inner world, to her creativity, and to the magic that exists within all of us. The Witching Hour, in the end, is not just a metaphor for the moment when Stevie Nicks tapped into her deepest creative powers, it is a symbol of her ability to transcend the ordinary and create something extraordinary, even when she was at her most vulnerable. Through her music, her image, and her spirituality, Stevie Nicks has shown the world that there is magic in the mundane and that it is possible to find strength in the moments of darkness.

Chapter 7: Edge of Seventeen

By the early 1980s, Stevie Nicks was no longer just a member of Fleetwood Mac. She had become a bona fide rock star, one whose name resonated just as deeply in the solo world as it did within the iconic band. The period following Rumours and the band's emotional upheaval saw Stevie finding her own voice and carving out a distinct identity beyond Fleetwood Mac's collective success. The transition from a member of a legendary band to a solo artist was not easy, but Stevie embraced it with the same passion and courage that had always defined her.

In 1981, Stevie Nicks released her debut solo album, Bella Donna, an album that would serve as a bridge between her work with Fleetwood Mac and her future as an artist on her own terms.

With its lush, layered sound and Stevie's signature mystical lyrics, Bella Donna was both a reflection of her past and a glimpse into her future. But it was the success of this album, along with the emotional depth of its songs, that propelled her into a new era of her career. However, it wasn't just the music that defined Stevie's solo career, it was also her ability to connect with her audience on a deeply personal level. As the years passed, it became clear that Stevie was not just the mystical "witch" of Fleetwood Mac but a voice of resilience, strength, and vulnerability.

In the midst of all this personal and professional transformation, a song was born that would come to define a moment in Stevie's solo career, and, by extension, her place in rock history: "Edge of Seventeen."

The story behind "Edge of Seventeen" is as much about loss as it is about triumph. In 1980, Stevie Nicks experienced two profound and heart-wrenching losses that would alter her life forever. First, she lost John Lennon, the iconic Beatle who had been tragically murdered in December 1980. For Stevie, Lennon's death felt personal, as his music had been a major influence on her during her formative years. Lennon was a figure whose artistry had shaped her view of music and the world, and his untimely death was a blow to Stevie that she couldn't fully process at the time. However, it wasn't just Lennon's death that devastated Stevie, it was also the passing of her uncle, Jonathan, who had been a major figure in her life. Uncle Jonathan had supported her music career and was someone she could always turn to for guidance and love. His death, shortly after

Lennon's, left Stevie reeling, grappling with the twin tragedies that had rocked her world.

It was in the midst of this grief that "Edge of Seventeen" was born. The song began as a reflection of Stevie's own sorrow, but it evolved into something more universal. "Edge of Seventeen" became a song about the experience of losing someone you love, about the sharp edges of grief that continue to haunt you long after the person is gone. The lyrics spoke to Stevie's own mourning but also touched a chord with anyone who had experienced the pain of losing a loved one.

"Edge of Seventeen" quickly became one of Stevie Nicks' signature songs, a track that still resonates deeply with fans to this day. The song's signature riff, which evokes both nostalgia and longing, is a defining feature of Stevie's solo work. But it's the emotional power of the song that has made it a lasting anthem for generations of listeners.

The song's chorus, "Just like the white-winged dove / Sings a song, sounds like she's singing / Ooh, baby, ooh, said ooh", captures both the mournful beauty of loss and the hope that comes with it. The white-winged dove, often interpreted as a symbol of peace, becomes a metaphor for the voices of the departed who live on in spirit. It's as if the song is trying to reconcile grief with the hope of healing, something Stevie herself was struggling to do in the wake of these losses.

What made "Edge of Seventeen" so powerful was its ability to transform personal grief into something universally relatable. Though it was inspired by Stevie's own pain, it became a song that spoke to everyone who had ever experienced the loss of a loved one. The mournful yet uplifting melody, combined with Stevie's soulful delivery, made it an anthem of resilience, a song that reminded people that even in the darkest moments, there is still light and hope to be found. As the song became a massive hit, Stevie's solo career continued to soar. The success of Bella Donna, and particularly "Edge of Seventeen," solidified her status as an artist in her own right. It was clear that Stevie Nicks wasn't just the woman behind Fleetwood Mac's hits, she was also an individual artist whose music spoke to deep, universal truths.

While "Edge of Seventeen" spoke to the vulnerability that Stevie felt in the wake of loss, it also marked a crucial moment in her evolution as an artist. The song showcased the duality that had always been a part of Stevie's identity, the juxtaposition of light and dark, of love and loss, of beauty and sadness. This duality was what made Stevie's music so compelling, her ability to embrace both sides of the emotional spectrum and create something that resonated with listeners on a profound level.

Stevie's persona as a mystical, ethereal figure was still central to her identity, but with songs like "Edge of Seventeen," she showed that she could also be deeply grounded in reality. She wasn't just the witch on stage, she was a woman who had lived, loved, and suffered, someone who knew the complexities of the human experience and was willing to confront those complexities head-on. "Edge of Seventeen" was a perfect encapsulation of this side of Stevie, her ability to channel personal experiences into something larger than herself, something that spoke to the collective.

The Song That Became a Cultural Touchstone

"Edge of Seventeen" became more than just a song, it became a cultural touchstone. Over the years, it has been used in numerous films, TV shows, and commercials, solidifying its place in pop culture. The song's haunting riff, Stevie's soaring vocals, and the raw emotion behind the lyrics have made it a timeless classic.

For Stevie Nicks, "Edge of Seventeen" was not just a career milestone, it was a reflection of her strength and resilience as an artist. It was a moment when she was able to take her personal pain and transform it into something that would live on long after her grief had subsided. It was the song that defined a new chapter in her solo career, one that would see her rise to even greater heights.

Even now, decades later, "Edge of Seventeen" continues to be one of Stevie Nicks' most beloved songs. It's a reminder of the emotional depth that she brings to her music and the lasting impact her art has had on her fans. In a career that has spanned over five decades, "Edge of Seventeen" remains a testament to Stevie's ability to speak to the heart of the human experience, to capture grief, loss, and hope in a way that transcends time. As Stevie Nicks moved forward with her solo career, "Edge of Seventeen" became the song that anchored her legacy. It was a song that not only defined her early solo years but also encapsulated everything that made her unique as an artist. With her deeply personal lyrics, ethereal stage presence, and ability to tap into universal emotions, Stevie Nicks became a solo artist whose influence stretched far beyond Fleetwood Mac.

But "Edge of Seventeen" also marked the beginning of a new era for Stevie, a time when she could step out from the shadows of Fleetwood Mac and explore her own creative boundaries.

The success of the song proved that Stevie was not just a band member but a solo artist in her own right, with a voice and vision that would carry her far beyond the limits of her previous successes.

Chapter 8: Love, Loss, and Leather and Lace

Stevie Nicks has always been a paradox: a woman of immense strength and deep vulnerability, a lover and a loner, an artist who could pour her heart into music while simultaneously wrapping it in layers of mystery and mysticism. Love, in all its forms, has played a pivotal role in shaping Stevie's music, her persona, and her journey through life. However, it has also been the source of great pain and profound loss. Throughout her career, Stevie has written some of the most poignant songs about love, both the exhilarating highs and the devastating lows. Among the many songs Stevie wrote and performed, "Leather and Lace" stands out as a profound reflection of love and loss. Released as a single in 1981 from her debut solo album Bella Donna, "Leather and Lace" marked a defining moment in Stevie's career as a solo artist. But the song's power goes beyond its success, it encapsulates the deep emotional currents that ran through Stevie's life, capturing both her vulnerabilities and her resilience.

"Leather and Lace" is one of Stevie Nicks's most beloved and enduring songs, but its origins are tied to both personal heartache and professional collaboration. The song was written as a reflection of Stevie's emotional state in the wake of a difficult breakup, but it was also a moment of artistic collaboration with one of her closest friends and a fellow musician, Don Henley of the Eagles. Henley's gravelly voice blended perfectly with Stevie's ethereal tones, creating a harmonic balance that gave the song a timeless quality. At its core, "Leather and Lace" is about the complexity of relationships, the push and pull of love, the contradictions that arise when two people who are both strong and fragile come together. The lyrics are raw and vulnerable, speaking to the delicate dance between needing someone and learning to let them go. The title itself is symbolic, representing the juxtaposition of hard and soft, of toughness and vulnerability, two qualities that Stevie, and her music, have always embodied. "I'm just a bird in a gilded cage," Stevie sings at the beginning of the song, evoking a sense of confinement and longing, yet also implying a sense of beauty and privilege. It's a powerful image of a woman who feels both trapped and adored, whose heart is both free and bound by the forces of love and loss. The combination of "leather" (representing toughness) and "lace" (representing softness and fragility) is a perfect metaphor for Stevie's duality, she was both a powerful force and a woman full of delicate emotions. The creation of "Leather and Lace" was not only an artistic collaboration but also a testament to the closeness that Stevie Nicks and Don Henley shared, both as artists and as friends. Their relationship was marked by mutual respect and admiration, and while their romantic lives were complicated, the bond they shared was rooted in shared experiences and deep emotional connection. Henley's voice on the track, with its deeper, more grounded tone, complements Stevie's high, lilting voice in a way that perfectly embodies the dualities within the song itself. However, while "Leather and Lace" is often seen as a beautiful love song, it is also a reflection of the emotional realities Stevie was living through at the time. The early 1980s were a period of turmoil for Stevie, both personally and professionally. The end of her relationship with her longtime partner, Lindsey Buckingham of Fleetwood Mac, was still a fresh wound, and she was dealing with the emotional fallout of that breakup. Additionally, the demands of being a solo artist were beginning to take their toll. "Leather and Lace" became a way for Stevie to channel the complexities of her emotions into something tangible and relatable.

Loss was a theme that pervaded much of Stevie's music, and "Leather and Lace" was no exception. The song can be interpreted as a reflection on the vulnerability of love, particularly love that is tinged with sorrow and unspoken regret. In the line "It's just a dream, you know / You could stay or you could go", Stevie speaks to the uncertainty that often accompanies relationships, whether it's the fear of abandonment or the overwhelming desire to hold on. The choice between staying or leaving becomes a delicate one, and the song captures that tension beautifully. For Stevie, love was never a simple matter, it was always intertwined with loss, both romantic and personal. Her love life has been marked by heartbreak and longing, often punctuated by the dissolution of relationships that she held dear. The pain of these losses has been a source of much of her inspiration, and "Leather and Lace" is an example of how she could take personal sorrow and transform it into something profoundly beautiful. Stevie has often spoken about the deep sadness that accompanied her breakup with Lindsey Buckingham, a relationship that had been central to her identity both as a person and as an artist. The emotional complexities of their relationship were expressed not only in the music they made together but also in the way their personal lives intertwined with Fleetwood Mac's success. The emotional toll of their breakup, however, was not something Stevie could easily escape. She poured this sorrow into her solo work, and "Leather and Lace" became a vehicle for her to express her vulnerability in a way that was honest yet beautifully composed.

In the years following the release of "Leather and Lace," Stevie Nicks found herself going through a period of self-discovery. She was no longer just the mystical, ethereal figure of Fleetwood Mac, she was a solo artist, learning to navigate her own emotional landscape while dealing with the pressures of fame, addiction, and the complexities of her relationships. "Leather and Lace" became a kind of personal anthem, a reminder that even in the face of loss, love could still be transformative.

As Stevie's solo career continued to evolve, she embraced the idea of transformation and reinvention. She was no longer the young woman who had written songs about heartbreak in the early days of Fleetwood Mac, she was a seasoned artist, someone who had lived through the highs and lows of fame, love, and loss. Yet, in songs like "Leather and Lace," she was still able to capture the raw emotion of the past and weave it into a new artistic narrative.

"Leather and Lace" remains one of Stevie Nicks' most enduring songs, a testament to her ability to capture the essence of love and loss in a way that speaks to listeners across generations. The song's timeless appeal lies in its raw emotional honesty and the way it blends Stevie's poetic sensibilities with the universal themes of love, longing, and heartbreak. Its impact has been felt not only by Stevie's fans but also by musicians and artists who have drawn inspiration from its intricate songwriting and emotional depth. Over the years, "Leather and Lace" has been covered by countless artists, further cementing its place in the pantheon of classic rock ballads. Stevie's voice, still as haunting and powerful as ever, continues to resonate with audiences, proving that the song's message about love's complexities is timeless. It is a song that speaks to the heart of what it means to be human, full of contradictions, full of passion, and always searching for connection.

In the end, "Leather and Lace" is more than just a song, it's a reflection of Stevie Nicks's journey through love, loss, and self-discovery. It captures the dualities that have always defined her as both an artist and a woman, the strength and vulnerability, the independence and longing, the toughness and tenderness. The song is a reminder that love, no matter how painful, is an essential part of the human experience and that even in our darkest moments, there is beauty to be found.

Stevie Nicks continues to be a symbol of resilience, and "Leather and Lace" stands as one of her most poignant and beloved songs. It encapsulates not only the complexities of love but also the enduring power of Stevie's artistry, the ability to take personal experiences and transform them into something that resonates with everyone who has ever experienced the highs and lows of love.

Chapter 9: Dances with Demons

The life of Stevie Nicks is one marked by both extraordinary highs and profound lows. From the glamor of superstardom to the darkness of personal struggles, Stevie has lived a life that has been anything but ordinary. Behind her mystical persona and iconic music, there were moments of deep despair, periods when the bright lights of fame seemed distant, and when the demons that lurked in the shadows threatened to consume her. But it was through these challenges, particularly her battle with addiction, that Stevie Nicks truly learned to rise above the darkness and transform her pain into artistry.

Stevie's journey through addiction wasn't something she shied away from acknowledging.

In fact, she has often spoken candidly about the pressures of fame, the emotional toll it took on her, and the ways in which she used substances to cope with the emotional chaos that accompanied her rock-and-roll lifestyle. The 1970s and 1980s were a time when drugs and alcohol were deeply embedded in the culture of rock music, and Stevie, like many of her peers, was drawn into that world. But it was during these turbulent years that Stevie experienced some of her greatest challenges, and ultimately, her most significant personal and artistic reinventions.

In the early days of Fleetwood Mac's success, Stevie Nicks was at the center of a whirlwind of fame, touring, and recording. She was living the rock-and-roll dream, surrounded by music, adoration, and the intoxicating allure of the lifestyle. But with fame came immense pressure, the pressure to perform, to be perfect, and to constantly live up to the expectations of fans, the media, and even herself. For someone like Stevie, who had always poured her heart into her music and her relationships, the constant demands of the spotlight began to take a toll.

The excesses of the rock-and-roll world, the late nights, the parties, and the easy access to drugs, were something Stevie, like many musicians, found herself caught up in. In her memoir and various interviews, she has been open about her struggles with cocaine addiction during the height of her career. It wasn't just the allure of fame or the thrill of the moment that led her down this path, it was also the emotional pain she carried with her, stemming from the personal turmoil she was experiencing in her relationships and her struggles with her identity as an artist.

Her relationship with Lindsey Buckingham, which had been a cornerstone of Fleetwood

Mac's creative output, was falling apart, and the emotional fallout from that breakup was devastating. This emotional devastation fueled her addiction, and she began to rely on substances as a way to numb the pain and escape the overwhelming emotions that accompanied her personal and professional life. The sense of loneliness that often came with fame, combined with the pressure to maintain her image and her role in Fleetwood Mac, made it even harder to cope. Stevie's addiction was not something that happened overnight, it was a slow burn that crept into every aspect of her life. During Fleetwood Mac's extensive tours, she found herself using cocaine regularly, often relying on it to maintain her energy levels and to stay in control amidst the chaos. But as her dependency grew, so did the consequences. The drugs not only took a toll on her physical health but also began to affect her relationships with the people closest to her, including her bandmates and family. As her drug use increased, Stevie began to lose control. She described moments of clarity, where she realized how much the addiction was affecting her, but those moments were fleeting, and the next high would soon cloud her judgment. The pressures of being a rock star, combined with the emotional turmoil of her personal life, made it incredibly difficult for Stevie to break free from the cycle of addiction. During this period, Stevie was also battling feelings of inadequacy. Despite the massive success of Fleetwood Mac and her solo career, she felt isolated and unsure of herself. The expectation that she should be constantly creative and productive added to the pressure. Her self-worth became tied to her success, and the fear of losing that success fueled her addiction even further.

The turning point for Stevie came when the consequences of her addiction became too severe to ignore. In 1986, after years of battling addiction, Stevie suffered a breakdown. She had been living in a constant state of chaos, torn between her creative spirit and the destructive forces of addiction. It was at this point that she realized she needed help. She had reached a crossroads: either she would continue down this destructive path, or she would face her demons and make the difficult choice to fight for her life. With the support of her bandmates, friends, and family, Stevie entered a rehabilitation center. She was determined to reclaim her life and her music, but it wasn't an easy journey. Overcoming addiction was not just about kicking the substance, it was about confronting the deep emotional scars that had driven her to seek solace in drugs in the first place. It was about learning to live without the crutches of substance abuse and finding a healthier way to cope with the emotional pain that had fueled her for so long. Stevie has often spoken about how difficult her time in rehab was, and how she had to confront her darkest fears and insecurities. But it was also during this time that Stevie began to rediscover herself, not just as a rock star, but as a person. For the first time in a long time, she was able to see herself clearly, without the haze of drugs clouding her perception.

The time Stevie spent in rehab marked the beginning of her transformation. It wasn't an instant fix, addiction is a lifelong battle, and Stevie has acknowledged that there were times when she relapsed. However, she learned the tools she needed to begin the long road to recovery. Her return to music was a reflection of this new chapter in her life. Stevie Nicks had been through the depths of despair, but she had emerged stronger and more grounded, with a renewed sense of purpose.

Her recovery wasn't just about staying sober, it was also about reclaiming her artistry and her identity. After rehab, Stevie threw herself back into her music, but this time, there was a newfound sense of clarity and focus. She was no longer the woman lost in the haze of drugs; she was an artist in control of her craft, who had learned to live with the demons of her past while finding the strength to move forward.

One of the defining moments of this new era for Stevie came with the release of her 1989 album The Other Side of the Mirror. The album, while still infused with Stevie's mystical lyrics and soulful melodies, marked a departure from her earlier, more vulnerable work. It was a reflection of her growth and transformation, as she found new ways to channel her experiences and emotions into music that was both raw and empowering. Stevie Nicks' journey through addiction was a harrowing one, but it ultimately became a defining part of her story. It was through her battle with addiction that she learned the true meaning of strength, strength not just in her ability to create music, but in her ability to face the darkest parts of herself and emerge victorious.

As Stevie's career continued to evolve, she used her experiences to inspire others. She has often spoken openly about her struggles with addiction, hoping to encourage others who might be going through similar battles to seek help and find a way out of the darkness. Her story became a testament to the power of resilience and the possibility of redemption, showing that even the most difficult demons could be overcome with time, effort, and the will to change.

Stevie's willingness to confront her personal demons head-on also helped redefine her public image. She was no longer just the "witchy" figure of Fleetwood Mac's past, she was a woman who had faced some of the harshest realities of life and had come out on the other side stronger for it. Her openness about her addiction struggles has made her a role model for many, showing that recovery is not only possible but can lead to a rebirth of creativity and self-empowerment.

In the end, Stevie Nicks's story is one of triumph. Her dance with demons may have been long and arduous, but it was ultimately her resilience, creativity, and willingness to change that allowed her to overcome the darkness and embrace the light. Today, Stevie continues to be a symbol of hope, strength, and transformation, proving that even in the face of the most personal struggles, there is always a way to rise, reinvent, and emerge as something even more powerful than before.

Chapter 10: Enchanted Again

In the realm of rock music, few artists can claim to have captured the hearts and minds of listeners in the way that Stevie Nicks has. Her voice, both haunting and powerful, coupled with her lyrical ability to blend the mystical with the deeply personal, has made her a timeless figure in the world of music. But like many artists, Stevie's career has had its ebbs and flows. Through the ups and downs, she has continued to find ways to reinvent herself and reconnect with the magic that first made her a beloved icon. Chapter 10, Enchanted Again, captures the essence of Stevie's journey back to her creative core, her return to the enchanted world of music and inspiration that has always been the heart of her artistry. By the early 1990s, after years of touring, recording, and enduring both personal and professional trials, Stevie found herself at a crossroads. She had already endured the demons of addiction, seen the ups and downs of Fleetwood Mac's tumultuous career, and experienced the transformative highs of her solo success. Yet, in the midst of all her accomplishments, Stevie had begun to feel something was missing. The magic that had once fueled her songwriting and performances felt distant, like a dream that was slipping through her fingers. But as always, Stevie found a way to reinvent herself, turning to her past for the inspiration that would lead her to her next phase of creative brilliance. Stevie's return to her musical roots was a journey of self-discovery, a quest to find that spark of enchantment that had originally drawn her into the world of music. It began, ironically, in the least likely of places:

within herself. After years of fighting personal demons, enduring the grind of a relentless touring schedule, and navigating the ever-changing dynamics of Fleetwood Mac, Stevie needed to reconnect with the core of who she was as an artist. She started with a focus on writing. As the lyrics flowed, so did the sense of magic. The same inspiration that had guided her to pen songs like "Rhiannon" and "Landslide" began to resurface. Stevie had always drawn from the spiritual and mystical elements of life, blending the personal with the ethereal to create songs that resonated deeply with listeners. But after years of struggling with addiction and personal pain, she realized that her creative well had run dry. It was time to rebuild, to look inward, and find the emotional and spiritual energy needed to fuel her artistry once more. During this time, Stevie began to embrace the quieter, more introspective moments of her life, taking time to travel, reflect, and reconnect with her deep love for nature. Her experiences in the wilderness, especially her time in the deserts of California, served as a source of inspiration. She would often speak about how the natural world, with its vast expanses and infinite beauty, allowed her to heal. It was through this reconnection to herself and the earth around her that Stevie rediscovered the magic that had first inspired her music. She was no longer just the woman known for her iconic persona, she was once again Stevie Nicks, the poet, the dreamer, and the creator. In 2001, Stevie Nicks released Trouble in Shangri-La, an album that would mark her official return to solo work after a significant hiatus. The album, which was widely praised by both critics and fans, signaled Stevie's return to form, as she rekindled the magic that had made her a star in the first place. Among the tracks that stood out was "Enchanted," a song that captured the essence of Stevie's journey back to herself. "Enchanted" was a love letter to the past, to the dreams that had once felt so real, and to the sense of wonder that had always existed within her. The song was steeped in the same mystical imagery that had defined much of her early work, while also revealing a newfound clarity and sense of peace. "I'm enchanted, I'm enchanted by you," she sings, her voice full of longing, hope, and wonder. The song became an anthem for many fans who had followed Stevie's journey through the years, resonating with those who had witnessed her struggles and were now seeing her return to her true self. The song's success wasn't just about its beauty, it was about what it represented: a new chapter in Stevie's life, one where she had come to terms with the past and was looking forward to the future. In a sense,

"Enchanted" marked Stevie's artistic resurrection, signaling that she was ready to once again dance with the muses that had first inspired her. While Stevie was embracing her solo career with newfound vigor, the pull of Fleetwood Mac, the band that had launched her into stardom, was never far behind. In 1997, Fleetwood Mac reunited for a highly successful tour, and in 2003, they released Say You Will, their first album together in over a decade. For Stevie, this was another opportunity to revisit the creative magic that had originally brought her into the band, and it provided a fresh context for the songs she was writing at the time. However, this time around, the dynamic within Fleetwood Mac was different. The ghosts of past relationships, particularly with Lindsey Buckingham, still loomed large. The band's chemistry, once defined by its tumultuous romantic entanglements, had shifted, but the bond between the members was still there, and the music reflected that complex mix of emotions. Stevie's contributions to Say You Will and the subsequent tours allowed her to continue to stretch her artistic wings, balancing her solo work with her role in Fleetwood Mac. The tour gave her the chance to experience the magic of the band's legacy in front of sold-out audiences, allowing her to reconnect with her fans and with the music that had shaped her career.

But even with the success of Fleetwood Mac's reunion, Stevie's work as a solo artist remained her primary focus. She continued to embrace the freedom of creating music on her own terms, unencumbered by the pressures of band dynamics. "Enchanted" was not just a song for her, it was a statement of her independence, of her ability to stand alone and create magic on her own terms. One of the most profound aspects of

Stevie's return to her music during this time was her rediscovery of her voice, both literally and figuratively. Having spent so much of her career navigating personal struggles and the pressures of fame, Stevie had at times felt disconnected from her voice as an artist. But by the time she released Trouble in Shangri-La, she had fully reclaimed that voice. Her singing was as powerful as ever, and she was once again able to channel the raw emotion and poetry that had made her such a singular force in rock music.

In addition to rediscovering her vocal abilities, Stevie also reconnected with her role as a songwriter. The lyrics of "Enchanted," along with the songs on Trouble in Shangri-La, revealed a deep introspection, a reflection on the journey she had taken and the person she had become. Stevie had learned to embrace her imperfections, recognizing that it was her flaws, her struggles, and her resilience that had made her art so compelling. Stevie Nicks' return to music in the early 2000s wasn't just a comeback, it was a reinvention. Trouble in Shangri-La was a testament to her ability to evolve while staying true to the essence of what made her an icon in the first place. "Enchanted" was not only a celebration of her personal and creative rebirth, it was also a reminder that the magic of music, much like the magic of life, is never truly lost. It is always there, waiting to be rediscovered.

The song became a fan favorite, and as Stevie continued to tour, she found herself re-energized, able to perform with the same passion and intensity that had defined her early years in Fleetwood Mac. Her fans, those who had supported her through the highs and lows, welcomed her back with open arms. And in turn, Stevie was reminded of the power of connection, of the magic that exists when an artist and their audience share a moment of transcendence. Enchanted Again is more than just a chapter in Stevie Nicks' career, it is the embodiment of her resilience, her ability to reinvent herself, and her unwavering commitment to the magic that fuels her art. Through the years, Stevie has remained a woman enchanted by the world around her, by the music she creates, and by the endless possibilities of what can happen when an artist allows themselves to fully embrace the journey.

Chapter 11: Sister of the Moon

There is a quiet magic in the way Stevie Nicks has shaped her persona. Beneath the flowing shawls, the twirling skirts, and the glittering stage presence, there has always been something deeper, something mystical. The very air around her seems imbued with the ethereal, and her connection to the supernatural and the spiritual world has always been central to who she is as an artist. If there's one symbol that has defined much of Stevie's mystique, it is the moon, specifically, the moon as an ancient, feminine, and guiding force. In this chapter, Sister of the Moon, we explore how Stevie Nicks' relationship with the moon has transcended mere symbolism, becoming an integral part of her identity and artistry.

For Stevie Nicks, the moon has never just been a celestial body in the sky; it has been a muse, a constant source of inspiration, and a symbol of both feminine power and vulnerability. From the earliest days of her career, she has referred to the moon as a guiding presence in her life, a force that has shaped her creative process and the way she views the world. It is not a coincidence that one of Fleetwood Mac's most beloved songs, "Sister of the Moon," was written during the band's Rumours era, capturing the profound influence the moon has had on her.

The moon, in all its phases, holds a special place in Stevie's heart and in her songwriting. Much like the waxing and waning of the moon, Stevie's career has had its phases of growth, retreat, and reinvention. She has always viewed herself as being in tune with the moon's cycles, attuned to the subtle rhythms that govern both her personal life and her music. The moon has often represented a source of feminine power and independence in her songs, traits that are central to Stevie's own identity. Written by Stevie Nicks and featured on Fleetwood Mac's iconic 1979 album Tusk, "Sister of the Moon" is more than just a song; it is an ode to the moon itself, a reflection of Stevie's connection to the mysterious and powerful forces that guide her. The lyrics of the song speak to a kind of celestial kinship, as Stevie acknowledges a sisterly bond with the moon, a bond that feels at once protective, illuminating, and transformative.

In interviews, Stevie has explained that she wrote the song at a time when she was struggling with a tumultuous relationship, yet finding solace in the moon's steady, unchanging presence. The line, "Sister of the moon, I know you well" reflects Stevie's understanding of the moon as both a nurturing and a distant force, something she can rely on for comfort and guidance, even if it's not always in a tangible way. The imagery in the song speaks to the ways in which the moon represents a reflection of both the light and dark aspects of the feminine spirit. It embodies the duality of strength and vulnerability, which are qualities Stevie often explores in her own life.

When Stevie sings, "And I am your child," it speaks to a kind of intimate relationship with the moon, one that goes beyond simple admiration. It's a relationship built on a shared understanding of the cycles of life, birth, growth, loss, and renewal. For Stevie, this connection is deeply personal, and she has often spoken about how the moon's light, especially during moments of loneliness or uncertainty, has helped her navigate her own emotional landscape.

Stevie Nicks has long been associated with a certain spiritual mystique, a sense that there is more to her than meets the eye. It's not just about her wardrobe of flowing scarves and mystical imagery; it's about a deep-rooted belief in the power of the unseen. The moon, as a symbol of feminine mysticism, has been a guiding force in Stevie's life, representing the sacred and the mysterious.

The concept of femininity has been a constant thread in Stevie's music and identity. From the beginning of her career, she embraced the idea of women being powerful, complicated, and full of contradictions. The moon, with its ever-changing face, reflects this idea of feminine complexity, how a woman can be both a source of light and shadow, nurturing and fierce, delicate and strong. Stevie's fascination with the moon goes beyond its physical beauty; it represents the divine feminine, the unseen forces that drive creativity, intuition, and inner strength.

In her personal life, Stevie has often embraced these qualities, not just as an artist, but as a woman who has navigated the ups and downs of relationships, career, and self-discovery. For Stevie, the moon has served as a kind of silent witness to her journey. When she has struggled, she has turned to the moon for solace. When she has triumphed, she has thanked the moon for illuminating her path.

The moon's influence can be seen in some of Stevie Nicks' most beloved songs, where themes of light and darkness, love and loss, and the ethereal and earthly are explored. Whether in her solo work or with Fleetwood Mac, the moon has been a constant source of inspiration.

Songs like "Rhiannon," "Landslide," and "Edge of Seventeen" feature imagery of nature, the stars, and the moon, creating a sense of the mystical that is uniquely Stevie's. In "Rhiannon," for example, the lyrics describe a woman who is both mysterious and powerful, a figure that could be interpreted as a personification of the moon's own elusive nature. Rhiannon is described as a woman who "rings like a bell through the night," much like the moon rings through the silence of the night sky, guiding those who are willing to listen.

In Landslide, there's a subtle connection to the moon's cycles, with Stevie reflecting on the passage of time and the inevitable changes that come with it. The line "I've been afraid of changin' / 'Cause I built my life around you" resonates with the moon's ability to be both constant and yet ever-changing, offering a mirror to Stevie's own experiences of transformation and growth.

The moon also plays a symbolic role in Stevie's writing about love, loss, and healing. In "Silver Springs," for example, the imagery of the moon is intertwined with themes of regret and emotional release. The line "I'll follow you down 'til the sound of my voice will haunt you" speaks to a kind of haunting, a love that lingers in the darkness, much like the moon's silent watch over the earth. In addition to the moon's symbolic connection to the feminine and mystical, Stevie Nicks has long been associated with the occult and the spiritual. Her embrace of tarot cards, astrology, and other mystical practices has added layers to her public persona, enriching the already magical aura surrounding her. While some have seen these practices as mere performances or as part of her stage persona, for Stevie, they represent a deep belief in the unseen forces that guide her and influence her art. The moon, in particular, holds significance in many esoteric traditions. It represents intuition, the subconscious, and the cycles of life, ideas that resonate deeply with Stevie's own journey. Her connection to the occult is not about literal witchcraft, but rather about tapping into a deeper understanding of the world, one that recognizes the interconnectedness of all things, both seen and unseen. For Stevie, the moon serves as a constant reminder that there are forces beyond the material world that shape her art and her life. It is through her connection to these forces, whether through her music, her lyrics, or her spiritual practices, that Stevie has been able to maintain her creative spark for so many decades.

The Moon as a Metaphor for Stevie's Evolution

The moon is a powerful metaphor for Stevie Nicks' evolution as both an artist and a woman. Just as the moon goes through its phases, waxing, waning, and illuminating the night sky in different ways, Stevie's career has also gone through different cycles. In the early days of Fleetwood Mac, she was a rising star, illuminated by the light of the music world. As the years went on, she faced periods of darkness and uncertainty, but always, like the moon, she found her way back to the light. The moon's cycles represent the eternal ebb and flow of creativity and life. As Stevie's career continued to evolve, so did her relationship with the moon. She learned to embrace her own cycles of creativity, understanding that there would be moments of quiet reflection, as well as times of intense output. Her connection to the moon became a reminder that, like the phases of the moon, there is always a time for renewal and rebirth. "Sister of the Moon" is more than just a song, it is an anthem for the mystical, for the feminine, and for the cycle of life itself. In this chapter, we've explored how Stevie Nicks' personal connection to the moon has shaped her artistry, spirituality, and identity. The moon has been her guiding star, both in her darkest moments and in her brightest. It is a constant reminder that, like the moon, she is both ever-changing and eternal.

Chapter 12: What Made Stevie Nicks Stevie Nicks?

Stevie Nicks is an enigma. She is a mystic, an artist, a poet, and a woman whose journey through fame, heartbreak, and self-discovery has captivated audiences for over five decades. But what is it that truly made Stevie Nicks the icon we know and love today? What are the defining qualities, both personal and professional, that have shaped her into one of the most influential artists in the world? In this final chapter, we reflect on the essence of Stevie Nicks, the layers of her personality, her artistry, and the forces that have guided her throughout her extraordinary career.At the core of what makes Stevie Nicks Stevie Nicks is her undeniable talent as a singer-songwriter. She has always been an artist first, a storyteller who weaves magic into every note she sings and every word she writes. Stevie's ability to craft songs that resonate deeply with her listeners is a cornerstone of her appeal. Whether she's singing about love, loss, or personal growth, her lyrics have always been rich with emotion and imagery, inviting her audience into a world of both vulnerability and strength. Her songwriting is deeply personal, often reflecting her own experiences and emotions, yet somehow universal in its themes. Songs like "Landslide", "Edge of Seventeen", "Rhiannon", and "Silver Springs" encapsulate the human condition in a way that transcends time. There's a poetic quality to her writing, one that brings to life the feelings of longing, introspection, and resilience. Her lyrics have often spoken to the unspoken, giving voice to the complex emotions that many of us feel but cannot always articulate.

Stevie's songwriting is also defined by its unique blend of folk, rock, and mysticism. Her voice, haunting, soulful, and unmistakable, has a way of cutting through the noise of the mainstream, delivering songs that feel timeless. It's a rare combination: the emotional depth of folk, the grit of rock, and the ethereal quality of mysticism. This blend has allowed Stevie to bridge genres and appeal to a wide range of listeners, from fans of classic rock to those who appreciate the softer, more introspective side of music. Stevie Nicks is as famous for her mystical persona as she is for her music. From the moment she stepped into the spotlight with Fleetwood Mac in the mid-1970s, her unique style and aura made her stand out. The flowing shawls, the long flowing hair, the bohemian aesthetic, these elements have become iconic representations of her mystique. But it's not just her physical appearance that exudes magic. It's the way she carries herself, the way she speaks of the world around her, and the sense of otherworldliness she brings to her music and performances. Her fascination with the occult, astrology, tarot cards, and the supernatural became key components of her public persona, but they were also deeply personal beliefs. Stevie has always embraced the idea that there are forces in the world beyond what can be seen or touched, and she has often spoken about how these forces have guided her both in her career and her personal life. Whether she's speaking of the moon, of fate, or of the spirits that guide her, Stevie Nicks has always embraced the mysteries of life, inviting her fans to do the same.

Her spiritual beliefs and interests have always been closely tied to her music. Many of her songs, such as "Rhiannon" and "Sister of the Moon", are drenched in mystical imagery, capturing her fascination with the unknown. To this day, Stevie continues to embrace this spiritual side of herself, believing that it gives her strength and clarity in an often chaotic world. While Stevie Nicks is often seen as an embodiment of strength, whether through her bold fashion choices, her commanding stage presence, or her ability to persevere in the face of personal and professional struggles, she has never shied away from displaying her vulnerability. If anything, it is this raw honesty that has made her so relatable to her fans.

Stevie's ability to be open about her personal struggles, including battles with addiction, heartbreak, and the challenges of being a woman in a male-dominated industry, has made her a symbol of resilience. Her willingness to share her deepest emotions with her audience has created a bond that is rare in the world of celebrities. For many fans, Stevie's music has been a source of comfort, a reminder that they are not alone in their own struggles. One of the most enduring qualities of Stevie Nicks is her ability to take her pain and turn it into art. Whether she's writing about a failed relationship, the loss of a friend, or the challenges of being a public figure, Stevie has always used her music as a cathartic outlet. It's this willingness to face her demons head-on and channel that energy into her art that has made her one of the most powerful and enduring voices in music history. Another key factor that has contributed to Stevie Nicks's legendary status is her ability to reinvent herself while staying true to her core identity. Over the decades, Stevie's career has seen countless reinventions, from her time with Fleetwood Mac to her solo work, to her return to the stage in recent years. Yet, through it all, she has remained unmistakably herself. Stevie's ability to evolve artistically while remaining true to her own unique voice is a rarity in the music industry. Whether she's experimenting with new sounds, collaborating with other artists, or shifting her public image, Stevie has always found ways to remain relevant and fresh while maintaining her distinct identity. She's not afraid to take risks, to try new things, or to explore different sides of her artistry. But at the same time, there's always an underlying consistency in her music, the same themes of love, loss, strength, and spirituality that have always defined her work.

This sense of reinvention is also reflected in Stevie's personal life. Over the years, she has faced numerous challenges, from the tumult of Fleetwood Mac's internal struggles to her personal battles with addiction, and yet, she has always managed to rise again, stronger and more determined. She has been open about the fact that she has reinvented herself time and time again, both in her music and in her life, but each reinvention has been a reflection of her ongoing growth as an artist and as a person. At the heart of what made Stevie Nicks Stevie Nicks is her unwavering commitment to authenticity. From the very beginning of her career, Stevie refused to conform to the typical expectations of the music industry. She was never interested in being a product of the commercial machine; instead, she was determined to carve out her own space in the world of music, one where she could be true to herself and her art. This authenticity is perhaps the most defining aspect of Stevie's career. In a world that often demands conformity, she has remained fiercely independent, refusing to compromise her artistry or her beliefs. Whether it's through her hauntingly beautiful vocals, her deeply personal lyrics, or her commitment to exploring the mystical side of life, Stevie has always been unafraid to show the world who she truly is.

Her authenticity has resonated with millions of fans around the world, many of whom see in her a reflection of their own struggles, desires, and dreams. For those who have followed her for decades, Stevie Nicks is more than just a rock star, she is a symbol of independence, strength, and the power of embracing one's true self.

So, what made Stevie Nicks the icon she is today? It is the combination of her visionary artistry, her mystical persona, her vulnerability, her strength, and her unwavering authenticity. It is her ability to connect with her audience on a deeply emotional level, her dedication to her craft, and her refusal to conform to the expectations of the music industry. It is the way she has navigated the complexities of fame, love, loss, and personal growth with grace and resilience. Ultimately, what made Stevie Nicks Stevie Nicks is the unique alchemy of talent, spirit, and individuality that has shaped her into one of the most enduring and beloved artists in the world. She has transcended the role of a mere musician and become a cultural icon, whose influence stretches far beyond music. Stevie Nicks is not just a singer or a songwriter; she is a symbol of artistic freedom, personal growth, and the power of embracing the mysterious forces that guide us all. As we look back on her incredible journey, one thing is clear: Stevie Nicks has not only made an indelible mark on music history, but she has also paved the way for generations of artists to embrace their own individuality and follow their own path. And in that, she has truly become the Sister of the Moon, guiding us all through the ever-changing cycles of life.

Epilogue

As we reach the final pages of What Made Stevie Nicks Stevie Nicks?, it becomes clear that Stevie's story is far from over. Though she has lived an extraordinary life, filled with both highs and lows, triumphs and tragedies, her impact continues to grow. She remains a beacon of artistry, individuality, and resilience—a true legend whose influence is felt not only in the world of music but across the entire cultural landscape. To understand the magnitude of Stevie Nicks' legacy, we must look beyond the accolades and the chart-topping hits, into the deeper, more lasting aspects of her artistic and personal journey. One of the most remarkable aspects of Stevie Nicks's career is her ability to transcend generations. In an industry that is often quick to move on from its stars, Stevie has remained relevant, admired, and beloved by both her original fans and a new generation of listeners. This phenomenon is not accidental; it is the result of her profound ability to connect with people on a deeply emotional level.

From the moment she stepped into the spotlight with Fleetwood Mac in the mid-1970s, Stevie's voice became a symbol of both strength and vulnerability. Her haunting, ethereal vocals spoke to the hearts of listeners, offering a unique blend of emotional depth and mysticism. This voice, coupled with her vivid storytelling, allowed her to craft songs that felt timeless. Tracks like "Landslide", "Rhiannon", and "Edge of Seventeen" became anthems for generations of fans.

However, it is not only her music that keeps her voice alive. Stevie Nicks has managed to remain a cultural touchstone, influencing musicians, songwriters, and even fashion designers. The bohemian look, once a hallmark of her style, has influenced countless trends, while her unapologetic individuality has inspired countless others to follow their own path. For many, Stevie Nicks is not just a musician, she is a symbol of what it means to be true to oneself in an often superficial world. Stevie's ability to remain both timeless and relevant is also a testament to the universal themes present in her music. Love, heartbreak, self-discovery, and empowerment, these are topics that will always resonate with people, regardless of when they first hear her songs. As long as her music continues to be played on airwaves, as long as new fans continue to discover the magic of Fleetwood Mac or her solo work, Stevie's voice will remain as powerful and relevant as ever.

Stevie Nicks' journey is one marked by personal growth and, perhaps more importantly, reinvention. Over the years, Stevie has weathered many storms, losing close friends, battling addiction, facing the complexities of fame, and enduring the heartbreak of failed relationships. Yet, time and time again, she has emerged stronger, more self-aware, and even more committed to her artistry.

Her ability to transform herself, whether artistically, personally, or professionally, is one of the most defining aspects of her career. When Fleetwood Mac was at its height of fame in the late 1970s, the band was plagued by internal turmoil, fueled by romantic entanglements, personal conflicts, and substance abuse. And yet, out of this chaos emerged some of their most iconic music, including the record-breaking Rumours. The raw emotions that permeated that album reflected Stevie's personal struggles, but it also marked the beginning of her evolution as both an artist and a person.

Her solo career, which began in the early 1980s, is a perfect example of her continual reinvention. Stevie Nicks did not rest on her laurels as a member of Fleetwood Mac. Instead, she branched out, creating music that was both deeply personal and experimental, exploring different musical styles while staying true to the essence of who she was. It was a bold move at a time when many artists feared breaking away from their established success. But Stevie was never one to follow conventional paths. Her solo albums like Bella Donna and The Wild Heart allowed her to express her voice in new ways, establishing her as a force in her own right.

Even in the face of personal loss, be it the death of her beloved uncle Jonathan or the breakup of relationships that inspired some of her most famous songs, Stevie has continually reinvented herself, finding new meaning in the world around her. This ability to transform herself, to move through the painful chapters of her life with dignity and grace, is something that resonates with her fans. It's a reminder that, no matter how many obstacles we face, there is always the possibility of renewal, of rising again and forging ahead.

While much has been written about Stevie Nicks the artist, it's important to remember the woman behind the icon. Stevie has always been more than just the mystical, bohemian figure that we see on stage. She is a woman who has lived a full and complex life, one filled with love, loss, joy, sorrow, triumph, and tragedy.

Stevie's personal life has been marked by a series of intense relationships, romantic, platonic, and familial, that have shaped her deeply. The death of her best friend and confidante, Robin Snyder, had a profound effect on her. It was this loss that led Stevie to write the haunting "Silver Springs", a song that continues to capture the heartache of losing someone dear. Similarly, her turbulent relationship with Lindsey Buckingham, her musical partner and one of the most significant people in her life, was both a source of pain and inspiration. Despite the heartache, their creative partnership birthed some of Fleetwood Mac's most iconic songs. In many ways, Stevie Nicks has lived her life in the public eye, yet she has remained fiercely protective of her privacy. Throughout her career, she has been open about her struggles with addiction, particularly during the 1980s, when cocaine became an almost ubiquitous part of her life. Yet, she has also shown immense strength in confronting those demons, emerging as a role model for others battling similar issues. Her openness about her addiction has helped many fans find their own paths to recovery, and her advocacy for mental health and substance abuse awareness has further solidified her status as a beloved and relatable figure.

What sets Stevie Nicks apart from many other artists is the sense of authenticity she brings to her personal life. She has never tried to conceal her flaws or paint a perfect image of herself. Instead, she has embraced both her strengths and weaknesses, understanding that true power comes from embracing who we are, flaws and all. Her ability to remain true to herself, and to find meaning in her struggles and joys alike, is something that continues to inspire millions of fans worldwide.

In addition to her direct influence on her fans, Stevie Nicks has also left an indelible mark on countless other artists. From female rock stars like Sheryl Crow, Florence Welch, and Lana Del Rey to contemporary pop stars such as Harry Styles and Taylor Swift, many musicians have cited Stevie Nicks as an influence. Her blend of raw emotion, poetic lyricism, and unique stage presence has shaped a generation of artists who strive to carry forward the torch she lit.

Her influence is not just limited to music. The bohemian style she helped popularize in the 1970s has become a hallmark of fashion culture, inspiring designers, stylists, and everyday people to embrace their own sense of individuality. Stevie's fashion, flowing shawls, bell sleeves, lace, and velvet, became an emblem of freedom and self-expression, making her a style icon long before the term "influencer" existed.

Even more significant is the emotional and creative impact Stevie has had on other artists. Her ability to write songs that are both intensely personal and universally relatable has set the standard for songwriting in many genres. Her gift for expressing complex emotions, navigating love, pain, and self-discovery, has been a blueprint for other songwriters striving to capture the truth of human experience in their work. Looking toward the future, it's clear that Stevie Nicks's legacy is far from being defined by her past. Her voice continues to be a source of inspiration, and her music will undoubtedly continue to impact future generations. There are few artists whose influence transcends time, but Stevie Nicks is one of them. As she continues to perform, to write, and to share her gifts with the world, it's exciting to imagine what the next chapter of her story might look like.

Perhaps the most powerful testament to Stevie's enduring legacy is the impact she has had on the culture at large. She has become more than just a musician; she is a symbol of empowerment, resilience, and artistic freedom. Her willingness to embrace both her strengths and weaknesses has made her a role model for those navigating their own struggles and seeking their own paths to self-discovery.

As the years go on, Stevie Nicks will undoubtedly remain an integral part of the musical landscape. Her songs will continue to be played on radio stations, in living rooms, and at concerts. Her influence will be felt in the music of new artists, in the fashion choices of everyday people, and in the hearts of fans who continue to find solace and inspiration in her words.

Stevie Nicks is not just a musician or a cultural icon; she is a living legend. Her legacy is built on her artistry, her resilience, and her unwavering commitment to authenticity. Through her music, she has inspired millions, showing us that even in the face of adversity, we can find strength, beauty, and grace. What made Stevie Nicks Stevie Nicks is not just her voice or her songs; it is her soul, her spirit, and the indelible mark she has left on the world. And as long as her music continues to resonate with fans, as long as her influence continues to shape the artistic world, Stevie Nicks will remain one of the most enduring and beloved figures in music history. Hi

Printed in Great Britain
by Amazon